THE RAPTORS OF IOWA

A BUR OAK BOOK

Holly Carver, series editor

THE RAPTORS OF IOWA

Paintings by James F. Landenberger

Essays by Dean M. Roosa,
Jon W. Stravers, Bruce Ehresman, and Rich Patterson

UNIVERSITY OF IOWA PRESS, IOWA CITY

University of Iowa Press, Iowa City 52242
Text copyright © 2013 by the University of Iowa Press,
paintings © 2013 by the estate of James F. Landenberger
www.uiowapress.org
Printed in the United States of America

Design by Kristina Kachele Design, llc

All royalties for this book are being donated by the Landenberger family
to The Nature Conservancy and the Iowa Natural Heritage Foundation.

The University of Iowa Press is a member of Green Press Initiative
and is committed to preserving natural resources.

Printed on acid-free paper
LCCN: 2012948889
ISBN-13: 978-1-60938-166-0
ISBN-10: 1-60938-166-1

In honor of James F. Landenberger, 1938–2003

CONTENTS

Nature's Teacher by Rich Patterson 1

The Intensity of Its Gaze by Dean M. Roosa 5

The Raptors of Iowa by James F. Landenberger 17

Turkey Vulture 18

Osprey 20

Swallow-tailed Kite 22

Mississippi Kite 24

Bald Eagle 26

Northern Harrier 28

Sharp-shinned Hawk 30

Cooper's Hawk 32

Northern Goshawk 34

Red-shouldered Hawk 36

Broad-winged Hawk 38

Swainson's Hawk 40

Red-tailed Hawk 42

Ferruginous Hawk 44

Rough-legged Hawk 46

Golden Eagle 48

American Kestrel 50

Merlin 52

Gyrfalcon 54

Peregrine Falcon 56

Prairie Falcon 58

Barn Owl 60

Eastern Screech-Owl 62

Great Horned Owl 64

Snowy Owl 66

Northern Hawk Owl 68

Burrowing Owl 70

Barred Owl 72

Great Gray Owl 74

Long-eared Owl 76

Short-eared Owl 78

Northern Saw-whet Owl 80

The Spiral of Perfection by Jon W. Stravers 83

A Growing Appreciation for Raptors by Bruce Ehresman 97

THE RAPTORS OF IOWA

NATURE'S TEACHER

Rich Patterson

ABOUT A DOZEN people gathered at the Cedar Rapids Indian Creek Nature Center one warm May morning in the late 1980s. Equipped with walking shoes and binoculars, they set out birding under the guidance of Jim Landenberger. Although I had organized the walk, I'm only a mediocre birder at best, and I looked forward to learning from Jim.

The group filtered through a woodland bordering Indian Creek and emerged onto a prairie while ticking off species either seen or heard: kingfishers, orioles, grosbeaks, song sparrows, yellowthroats, and more.

Then a problem arose.

A small dark bird perched on a fence post twenty feet from the group. A member of the great tribe of birds I generically call LBB, or little brown bird, it was indistinctly marked. Normally LBBs flit around so fast that birders don't get much of a look at them, giving their leader an opportunity to simply say, "Not sure what it is. Didn't get a good look," and move on.

This bird, however, was accommodating. It calmly studied the group. Everyone had binoculars trained on it, and someone said, "Jim, what kind of bird is that?" Jim peered. The bird stretched. Someone else asked, "Is it a warbler?"

Although an accomplished birder, Jim, I could tell, was stumped. He didn't know what it was. His face flushed as he responded with a string of unintelligible stuttering that could only have been an expletive. The maddening LBB eventually became bored with us and winged off into the nearby brush. During the rest of the walk, Jim helped us correctly identify more than thirty-five species.

Jim's bird study began in childhood, matured in youth, and flowered into an impressive artistic career. His stuttering was life changing. Wishing to become a biology teacher, he enrolled at the University of Iowa only to have professors discourage him. "You can't be an effective teacher with a severe stutter," they stated. Those professors inspired Jim to become one of Iowa's most unconventional but most effective teachers of natural history, especially birds. His medium was not the spoken word. It was art.

In childhood, Jim was a doodler. Rarely far from a scrap of paper, he used his pencil to create visual magic. This love of images led to a long career as an advertising artist at the *Cedar Rapids Gazette*. Designing display ads for cars, chiropractors, banks, and boutiques may have satisfied his doodling passion but left him remote from the birds he loved.

Jim's evenings were spent in his home studio, painting birds with the dream of becoming a successful professional freelance wildlife artist. Helped and mentored by good friend and renowned Canadian wildlife artist J. F. (Fen) Lansdowne, Jim perfected his craft. Eventually he sold a painting. Then another. Then limited-edition prints of his original watercolors began selling.

Jim's dream became reality when, after winning the Iowa waterfowl stamp contest in 1973 with his painting of gadwalls, he became the first three-time winner of the Iowa outdoor stamp design contests. With those awards came celebrity status and more painting and print sales in the golden era of wildlife art. He left the *Gazette* in 1977 to devote his energy to art.

Jim's work promoted his other passions: conservation and teaching. His art communicated the deep commitment to the protection of nature that permeated the very fabric of his being. Through art he became an effective teacher and motivator. Scan a Landenberger painting and you will see birds, fish, or furry animals surrounded by leaves, grasses, seeds, and sky in utter accuracy. Viewing a Landenberger painting sparks a desire to grab a pair of binoculars, strap on boots, and head for marsh, woods, or stream.

Painting, teaching, and conservation became intertwined and motivated Jim to donate art to Ducks Unlimited, helping this noted organization raise money to protect and restore waterfowl habitat.

Following the first Earth Day in 1970, Jim was approached with a crazy idea by Cedar Rapidians B. B. Stamats and Jean O'Donnell. Their vision was to establish a place, close to town, where school kids and their families could enjoy and learn from nature. It would be Iowa's first nature center.

They had a problem. No money.

The fledgling Indian Creek Nature Center needed dollars to hire staff to develop a children's environmental education program. Jim created and donated a stunning original watercolor, *Backwater Woodies,* to the Nature Center and allowed charter members to receive a free limited-edition print of the painting. Hundreds joined, and over the next forty years nearly two million people, mostly children, have visited the Nature Center. The original *Backwater Woodies* remains on display in the center's sunroom.

Jim faced a dilemma common to many artists. What one likes to create isn't always what sells. The stark reality of paying bills often dictated his paintings' subjects. In the heyday of wildlife art these tended to be game birds, especially waterfowl and pheasants. As the Landenberger reputation grew, his subjects expanded to include chickadees, goldfinches, river otters, trout, and many other scaled, furred, and feathered species. He also designed pewter belt buckles and created a striking backdrop for a diorama in Macbride Hall on the University of Iowa campus.

Few birds caught Jim's notice as much as Iowa's great diversity of hawks, falcons, eagles, and vultures, collectively called raptors. An artistic goal became the creation of paintings of all Iowa's raptor species. Jim finished most of these richly detailed, handsome paintings by 1997, culminating in the publication of this book many years later.

In 1997 Jim, his wife, Toni, and their two grandchildren moved to Florida. Until his death in 2003, he enjoyed and painted southern species and ocean scenes, but his connections to Iowa remained strong.

News of his death brought sadness to the Nature Center and his many friends. But years after his deft fingers last guided a watercolor-filled brush, he continues to teach and inspire the people who enjoy and love his art. This book builds upon his legacy.

THE INTENSITY OF ITS GAZE

Dean M. Roosa

ALDO LEOPOLD said that he could not live without wilderness. I share that feeling about raptors. I would feel cheated had I not been able to capture and band migrating hawks or climb to raptors' nests and hold a helpless chick that would become a skilled predator. All youngsters so inclined should have the chance to see what I saw, capture and band hawks, enter into a hunter's liaison with a bird in falconry, or marvel at the predatory efficiency of a master of the night like the great horned owl.

My serious interest in birds began in the mid 1950s, when I took Martin Grant's field biology course at Iowa State Teachers College (now the University of Northern Iowa). However, my exposure to and interest in raptors began much earlier. Every day on our small farm near Lehigh, Iowa, when I was young, I noticed that our flock of chickens would suddenly scramble and hide under anything available in response to a certain sharp note from one of the flock. Soon I realized that this was triggered by the sight of a hawk so distant that it was not visible to me until after the initial fright note had sounded. This intrigued me because the chickens were so young that they had probably never seen a hawk previously. The word "instinct" meant nothing to me then, but I pondered the improbability.

Many years later, my wife, Carol, and I stepped out of the back entrance of our business in Ames to see rock pigeons sitting, hiding really, on the ground behind trash cans and under cars, sitting so tightly that we could have easily picked them up. I said that a peregrine falcon must surely be in the vicinity. Soon an immature female peregrine floated over the alley. Again this interested me because most of the pigeons were young of the year and had certainly never seen a peregrine, or any other raptor, previously. But by now the power of instinct was no mystery to me.

When I was about eight or nine, my brother and I saw a small hawk flitting about our farm. For some reason, now unimaginable to me, we grabbed our single-shot .22 caliber rifle and followed the bird toward the woods. An unlucky shot brought this bird tumbling from the top of a tree. I can still see every detail of the landscape, the weather, the time of day, the hickory tree standing alone on a slight knoll . . . everything. There I stood with a beautiful hawk dying in my hands. We had no way of learning the bird's identity, but much later I realized it was a male American kestrel, one of our truly exotic-looking birds. Later, when I trapped and banded kestrels as a hobby, this scene replayed for me each time I took one from the trap and held it before releasing it.

One late fall day at about this same time, I noted a stream of hawks floating past a wooded hillside above the Des Moines River. I went to an ancient dump rake where I could sit and observe this passage of birds. For several hours, until dusk arrived, a steady parade of birds emerged from behind the woodland—a sight I have never seen in central Iowa since. At one point a bird changed course and came speeding low over the ground to snatch a sparrow from among a flock in a bush a few feet from where I sat. Thinking back on this, I realize now that these were principally accipiters—Cooper's hawks and sharp-shinned hawks—surely the spectacular capture of the sparrow was achieved by a sharp-shin. Again I wondered how they knew where to go; what was their guiding light? I do remember that the following days brought deteriorating weather and strong winds. In retrospect, I now realize that what followed was probably the famous Armistice Day storm of 1940, which created conditions that urged a huge migration. I remember nothing of the blizzard, but everything of the hawks that poured out over the landscape on that raw day.

Also at about this time, I remember looking out our front window on a Sunday afternoon to see a large bird sitting on a chicken it had just killed. The scene was so lucid that years later I realized this was an adult northern goshawk. I remember the intensity of its gaze and the beauty of its blue back, and the scene comes back to me in great detail: the weather, the time of day, the couch where I was sitting, the oil-burning stove, everything.

THE RUSH OF WINGS, THE FEELING OF WILDNESS

Years later, around 1956, Martin Grant and Myrle Jones helped me obtain a federal bird-banding permit. Articles by Daniel Berger and Helmut Mueller had taught me how to construct bal-chatri traps to capture hawks. These were especially effective at trapping American kestrels, and this became my long-standing activity during migration. I also learned, by visiting their banding station, how to construct a bow net for capturing large migrating hawks. Dave Fulks taught me the basics of how to construct and align nets specially made for capturing the hawks that came to our lure.

This was truly my most exciting activity involving the natural world. To be able to capture migrating red-tailed hawks, Cooper's hawks, rarely a northern goshawk or a peregrine falcon. To be able to hold these noble birds in my hands for a few minutes while attaching the band, to witness the intensity of their gaze, to occasionally, in a moment of carelessness, feel the grip of their talons in my flesh. If I look carefully, I can yet see faint scars on my hands these thirty years later. When captured, red-tails lie in a bander's arms like a baby. A northern goshawk, on the other hand, emits an ear-splitting alarm call that hastens its release.

One of the most interesting hawk-banding days in my memory took place in the Loess Hills near Turin. The previous day, Steve Duecker and I had banded a beautiful Krider's red-tailed hawk, one of our most attractive hawks. The following day bad weather descended, and I went up to disassemble our banding station. But, among the falling snow and falling temperature, I found myself amid an abundance of hawks attempting to escape the sharp wind. Seeing this, I ran back to get a lure and some bands. I banded several, then caught a bird that puzzled me. I finally was sufficiently perplexed that I released it unbanded. Later, I concluded that it was an unusually plumaged immature, dark-phase Swainson's hawk.

Shortly after obtaining a banding permit, I launched, much by accident, a study of large raptors, mainly along the Boone and Iowa Rivers in north central Iowa, close to where I was teaching. One year red-tails nested very commonly in western Wright County, and I banded those that I could. The next year there were no nests in the area, but by that time I was hooked, and I expanded my search for nests to the Iowa River. Each spring for the next decade, I hiked along the river looking for nests, became good at climbing, and greatly looked forward each year to this activity. The major large raptor was, of course, the red-tail. The other large buteo was the Swainson's hawk—much more rare and with a slightly higher pitch to its voice. The large owl was the great horned owl.

Looking at records of recovered banded birds from my study, I was surprised at the dispersal of the young. One was recovered in Alabama in the late fall of the year of banding. Two were found in northern Minnesota, also late in the year of banding. These last two records really surprised me; I thought the young would stay in the vicinity of their nest until late summer, then slowly move south to follow the food supply. Two birds, banded in east central Iowa, were found in the vicinity of the nest about ten years later. This too was surprising: These two hawks had probably each made a prey kill every day for a decade.

Each visit to a red-tail nest is a memory: the tiny gray balls of fuzz at three days that became the defiant, beautiful birds of twenty-one days; the adults screaming overhead as I banded their young and the startling rush of wings as they dove past my head; the ever-present gentle wind on the nest and the feeling of wildness that the setting brought. This feeling of wildness remained even though I could often see the water tower of a nearby small town from the nest; once I could see the campus of a great university from the nest tree.

The bird that evoked a huge amount of respect from me was the great horned owl, one of the most efficient predators in our state. It begins nesting activities in late winter to assure peak migration activity—and thus peak food supply—when the young hatch. I was a very energetic birder at that time, waking at dawn just to enjoy birds and bird songs. Still, the horned owl would scoop me—every now and then I found sora or snipe, for example, in its nest that I had not yet detected. The adults were superb providers. I would find the owl nest, often an old red-tail nest, lined with the bodies of waterfowl or shorebirds to the point where I could not immediately see the young owls. (In an article entitled "To Babes Really Lost in the Woods," Paul Errington recommended that anyone lost and hungry should look for the nest of this owl to take advantage of its super-abundant food.)

I usually wore a heavy cap when banding young great horned owls, due to the adults' reputation for aggressively defending their nest and young. This paid dividends on one occasion. I normally face the adult owl as much as I can, as this seems to dissuade it from coming too close. This time, I was focused on the young owls and paid no attention to the adult. Suddenly the adult struck me full force in the back of my head. More startled than injured, I turned to find a nearly pure black owl a few feet away—the only example of melanism that I have ever encountered in this species. It appeared almost as a chunk of coal with two gleaming yellow dots for eyes. And my camera back in my car!

An event in 1973 heightened my already exalted respect for this predator. Someone east of the town of Nevada in Story County was felling trees, and two baby great horned owls were flung from a cavity when a tree was cut. Not knowing what to do, they brought the young owls to George Knaphus at Iowa State University. George, knowing my interest in raptors, brought the downy young to my office.

It was late afternoon, and I wanted to get the young back near their nest yet that day. I grabbed my climbing irons and what construction materials I could find, these being a peach crate and small boards and a hammer and nails. I erected the box in a tree about a hundred yards from the original nest tree and placed the young in this new nest. It was now dusk; I climbed down and hid in the shrubbery to see whether an adult would come in response to the hunger calls of the young. Soon an adult came to perch in the top of the tree, looked down at the crude nest, and left. I left too, knowing that I had done what I could, confident that the young birds would be fed yet that night.

That was early April, and perhaps you remember what happened in central Iowa on April 8, 1973? The worst blizzard, or nearly the worst, of the century struck the Upper Midwest. I was so sure the young owls had perished that I did not check on the crate nest for a week or so. When I did climb up to the nest, I was startled but pleased. There, in aggressive posture, were the two young, now nearly feathered out and appearing as healthy as any two young owls I had ever seen. You begin to understand my respect for this marvel of survival. This is an owl designed to live in Iowa. It surely nests in every county, in cavities of trees, in buildings, in old hawk nests, and even in a structure built for goose nesting in a marsh, according to Doug Harr, wildlife biologist for the state of Iowa.

Over the years I have had occasion to accept young horned owls that someone felt had been abandoned. Since I normally had my eye on a horned owl nest in my vicinity, I would take the young and place them with the nestling owls. Invariably the adult owl accepted the new youngsters and raised them, even though there was sometimes a marked difference in their development.

For about an hour after sunset, when the western sky is red, owls can often be seen silhouetted against this background. Several times, when driving during this period, I would say to a passenger that we would probably see a horned owl in the next mile or so. And each time we did.

RAPTORS IN EDUCATION AND IN ART

Teachers use as aids those resources they know best. I have found birds to be of great benefit in teaching. Raptors can be useful for teaching about their use as early warning systems in recent decades, their special adaptations for survival, the fundamentals of predation and the ways that poisons are concentrated up the food chain, and so on. I would sometimes trap and detain an eastern screech-owl in my classroom to demonstrate owls' special adaptation for silent flight. I would bring in a captive bird for falconry for close-up viewing. Most students had never had the opportunity to see a hawk up close or to have it sit on their gloved fist.

There is a great need and opportunity for student interaction with raptors through the rehabilitation facilities that are becoming more common in Iowa. Often birds injured to a point where a disability will not permit them to be released can serve admirably as ambassadors in the classroom.

Until recently, raptors have not shared in the popularity of wildlife art. Only lately have artists like Robert Bateman and Owen Gromme included raptors in their portfolios. In Iowa, Jim Landenberger made a huge effort to capture the essence of raptors in the details of his paintings. Jim would frequent the banding station with us for a hands-on experience with living raptors.

Waterfowl have always dominated the wildlife art scene. This is as it should be, since large numbers of game hunters participate in the hobby of waterfowl hunting, and amateur ornithologists can more easily view the waterfowl and shorebirds that congregate in wetlands. Because raptors are generally more solitary, special effort must be made to study them.

Hawks and owls have long been persecuted; only recently has their beneficial nature been realized. For instance, Iowa did not have a law protecting hawks and owls until July 1, 1970, and as late as 1953 Alaska had a bounty on bald eagles; this stopped with the repeal of the Territorial Bald Eagle Bounty Law. A conservation club in the town where I once taught gave bonus points for killing Cooper's hawks. Even today many people cannot reconcile the role of predation with their outlook on nature.

Some Iowa raptors probably need no assistance in maintaining healthy population levels. These include the red-tailed hawk and the great horned owl. I would normally put the screech-owl on this list, but my personal observations indicate that this species has declined markedly since my childhood; something is suppressing its mournful call. In more than thirty years, I have heard the tremulous call of this bird only once in the vicinity of my acreage near Ames, where it should be plentiful.

Other species, such as the bird hawks, need somewhat undisturbed woodlands for nesting and extensive woodlands during migration for night roosts and hunting grounds. In some respects, Iowa's woodlands are in better condition in recent decades than previously, due to decreased woodland grazing by cattle. I find the butcher blocks of accipiters—where these bird hawks pluck their prey—only when I am in deep woodlands.

Northern harriers and short-eared owls need native prairie for nesting. Because these species are normally too fussy to use a restored prairie for this purpose, they are doomed to be very rare in Iowa.

There is great good news for certain species. The bald eagle has made a startling incursion into Iowa and is showing that it does not need remote wild areas for nesting, as I had believed. This is probably the result of a selection of a new ecotype by the slow accretion of tolerant individuals and their offspring from the large wintering population along the Mississippi River bordering eastern Iowa.

Other species need help. The American kestrel has benefited greatly from the nest box program now in operation along interstate highways. The osprey is benefiting from a release program for hatchlings originating far outside Iowa, although there have been natural nestings in recent years. Given its high nest fidelity, this species should increase dramatically in the future in Iowa.

The peregrine falcon, likewise benefiting from a hacking program of captively raised young birds, is now recolonizing historic sites. This is a dream come true for most birders, since this falcon is high on the list of desirable sightings.

The barn owl release program met with limited success, principally because Iowa is on the very northern margin of its range. However, with the climate changing rapidly, Iowa may very well soon be within its "normal" nesting range.

These release programs, wherein birds raised in captivity are released into urban environments as well as historic sites, are labor-intensive and expensive and speak to the danger of a species becoming rare or moving to the edge of extinction. There is also the danger of a gene pool becoming so low in diversity that a species is unlikely to recover.

The nongame program of the Iowa Department of Natural Resources has been of great value in initiating programs that benefit certain species such as the peregrine, osprey, and barn owl. The Iowa Department of Transportation, cooperating with the Iowa DNR's kestrel nest box program, is also doing a great service. The U.S. Department of Agriculture's Conservation Reserve Program, if made permanent and funded, would benefit songbird and small mammal populations and thus move up the food chain to benefit raptors. The trend toward larger agricultural fields, with the attendant removal of grassy fence rows—such good habitat for small mammals—will have a negative effect on the prey base of open-field and edge-nesting raptors. I doubt that this trend can be reversed as the planet's population soars.

Much thought went into the production of a 1986 research publication by the Raptor Research Foundation that discussed raptor conservation in the next fifty years. This worthwhile publication, international in scope, provides a synthesis of conservation efforts and principles that can be utilized in the central United States.

Unfortunately, each year enough hawks and owls are injured to necessitate the formation of raptor rehabilitation services. Gladys Black, Iowa's Bird Lady, was an early supporter of helping injured birds heal. She inspired Beth Brown of Osceola to continue and expand her efforts, which continue today along with other energetic efforts. For example, Laurie Spencer of Osceola also performs rehabilitation services. Kay Neumann of Dedham formed SOAR, Saving Our Avian Resources, in 1999, which leads efforts to rehabilitate raptors in western Iowa. Institutionally and early on, the Macbride Raptor Center, a joint venture of the University of Iowa and Kirkwood Community College, was formed to provide both education and rehabilitation. The Wildlife Care Clinic at Iowa State University includes treatment of raptors. And under construction as I write this is the Iowa Wildlife Center with Marlene Ehresman as director. Located near Ledges State Park, it will treat all wildlife, including raptors.

ॐ

THE ALLURE OF FALCONRY

In my mind, the sport of falconry is not detrimental to raptor populations when practiced ethically. To a person, every falconer I have known has been a passionate conservationist, and the falconry community has been instrumental in learning the secrets of captive breeding to supply birds in reintroduction efforts, especially of the peregrine. Most falconers pride themselves on being able to keep their birds feather-perfect and as healthy as if they were living in the wild. This is no mean task, for it is so easy for a bird to break a tail feather when capturing game, and certain diseases easily affect captive birds. Iowa now has a well-regulated falconry program; beginners must serve an apprenticeship under a master falconer and have quarters inspected by state personnel.

For a number of years early each fall, I trapped a female red-tail to train in the sport of falconry. Technically I was an austringer, someone who flies short-winged raptors as opposed to those who fly long-winged falcons. I would hunt with her into late fall, when I would release her. These birds varied widely in their response to capturing game. Most were keen on rabbits, one relished chasing pheasants, but capture was rare. One was obviously a mouser and would fly to a tree or pole and search for mice, ignoring larger game.

I considered some raptors to be so noble in pose or in flight that I would travel long distances to observe them. I went regularly to a special place in Colorado where ranchers, knowing I was conservation-minded, would let me on their property where golden eagles and prairie falcons were known to nest. Bobcats, rattlesnakes, and barn owls were thrown in as bonuses. For a few days I could observe falcons with their graceful flight and eagles in pursuit of game. I once found an eagle nest with two perfectly healthy young, a somewhat unusual occurrence.

For years I attended meetings of the North American Falconers Association, where I met men and women who rearranged their lives so they could care for and hunt with their falcon or hawk. Their passion, knowledge, and conservation ethics were often greater than mine.

I can look back over half a century of observations and say that nothing in nature is as exciting as a hunting raptor.

ABOUT THIS BOOK

The objective of this book is to highlight the paintings of James Landenberger. Jim's passion for the natural world shines through these paintings in their fine detail, the mood they capture, the very pose of each bird he chose to illustrate. I have always considered his works to be somewhere between those of Robert Bateman and John James Audubon—the mood captured by Bateman, the detail captured by Audubon.

Although some taxonomists now believe that the vultures should be included in the Ciconiiformes and that the falcons are more closely related to parrots than to the hawks, we have chosen to retain the traditional interpretation of raptors in this book. Species are presented in phylogenetic order, as in many field guides and the American Ornithologists' Union "Check-list of North American Birds." Two species of accidental occurrence in Iowa, the black vulture and the boreal owl, are not illustrated.

ACKNOWLEDGMENTS

Despite my reverence for the birds, it is the people whom I meet along the way who, in the end, are more important. People like Jon Stravers with his great insights into red-shoulder biology, or an artist with such talent and compassion as Jim Landenberger, or an expert falconer like Bob Elgin, or people like Gene and Eloise Burns who took kestrel banding to new heights by banding them each month of the year, or Bob Anderson who gave us a peek into the daily life and travels of bald eagles, or Pat Schlarbaum and Bruce Ehresman whose efforts at introducing and reintroducing several raptor species are starting to pay dividends. These and other dedicated people have enriched my life and the lives of all wild things.

Before his death, Jim Landenberger prepared the following: "We dedicate this book to Dr. George Schrimper, director of the Natural History Museum, University of Iowa, Iowa City. George was most helpful lending study skins for use in preparing paintings, obtaining good models for those that were not readily accessible, and helping in every way in the preparation of the paintings. Should every artist be so fortunate as to have such a friend." I know Jim would still want George Schrimper's contribution to the book acknowledged.

THE RAPTORS OF IOWA

James F. Landenberger

TURKEY VULTURE

Cathartes aura

These common summer residents arrive in Iowa early in March; most are gone by mid October. They nest sparingly, mainly in south central Iowa. They form communal roosts, principally on wooded bluffs along major streams; some such roosts have been in continual use for decades. Carrion feeders, they are often seen feeding on roadkill and seem to be one of the few bird species that can locate decaying food by smell from a distance. The black vulture, *Coragyps atratus*, while still considered of accidental occurrence in Iowa, has become of nearly regular occurrence in the last decade. This may be due to increased interest in the sport of birding or to the rapid climate change that is causing so many southern species to inch farther north. Look for it to be seen on a regular basis. In the meantime, study flocks of turkey vultures for a bird with notably shorter tail feathers, shorter and wider wings, and light-colored primary feathers, especially near the tip of the wing.

OSPREY

Pandion haliaetus

The osprey is an uncommon migrant, appearing in Iowa from early April to mid May and again in August and September. A fish feeder, it depends on open water to initiate migration. Records are becoming more frequent in recent years due to introduction attempts by the Iowa Department of Natural Resources and many conservation partners. Iowa's first nesting attempt was in 2000, and twelve out of sixteen nesting attempts in 2011 produced young.

SWALLOW-TAILED KITE

Elanoides forficatus

Our most elegant raptor is now of accidental occurrence in Iowa. It once nested sparingly in the state but disappeared prior to the twentieth century. With its long, forked, barn swallow–like tail, it is unmistakable. There have been three records in modern times: Black Hawk County in 1992, Cerro Gordo County in 2000, and Johnson County in 2004.

MISSISSIPPI KITE

Ictinia mississippiensis

This graceful bird now regularly occurs in Iowa, being reported each year. It returned in 1978 after an absence of some seventy years. There are historic records of nesting in Iowa; in modern times, it has nested in Polk County in 1995 and succeeding years, and there is recent evidence of probable nesting in Ottumwa.

BALD EAGLE

Haliaeetus leucocephalus

What a remarkable story surrounds our national symbol in Iowa! The bald eagle seems to have disappeared from Iowa as a nesting species around 1905, reappearing in Allamakee County in 1977. Since then it has spread statewide, with the most recent nest count being approximately three hundred nests in ninety-three counties. It congregates near open-water sites along larger rivers, especially the Mississippi, where it feeds on fish and waterfowl. Young eagles are solid brown, achieving their white heads and tails around age four. The white feathers of the adult's head make this bird eminently recognizable (see page iii); its immaculate appearance, both regal and untamed, is a testament to its endurance as our national symbol. In recent years, the world has been able to watch nesting bald eagles via the popular Decorah eagle cam.

NORTHERN HARRIER

Circus cyaneus

There is no mistaking the characteristic flight of the northern harrier. It flies low over grasslands, quartering section by section. The white rump patch is a definitive field mark. A fairly common migrant, the harrier is most frequently spotted from mid March to mid April and again from mid September to mid October. It prefers native prairie for nesting; both habitat and bird are rare in Iowa.

SHARP-SHINNED HAWK

Accipiter striatus

This exciting accipiter is a common migrant, seen in Iowa from mid March to mid May. It is an uncommon winter resident and apparently a very rare nester, with newly fledged young being seen in western Iowa and in Hardin and Lucas counties in recent years. It may have been a fairly common nester prior to the twentieth century.

COOPER'S HAWK

Accipiter cooperii

The Cooper's is a fairly common migrant, an uncommon nester, and an uncommon winter resident. It nests most frequently in south central and northeast Iowa, but its secretive habits may help it escape detection in other parts of the state. Its flight pattern and coloration have long caused this accipiter to be called the blue darter. It preys almost exclusively on small birds, and the short, rounded wings and long tail of this and other accipiters equip it elegantly for pursuing prey in heavy vegetation, usually trees. At the last instant before hitting the net at a banding station, this bird may spread its wings and tail, nearly stop in midair, rise over the net, and drop on the lure. The young are streaked with brown; adults have a slate back and barred front.

NORTHERN GOSHAWK

Accipiter gentilis

The goshawk, the largest of the bird hawks, is a rare winter resident in Iowa, appearing in late September and leaving by mid April. Periodically, the food base of this northern species declines, causing a southward invasion into neighboring states. Watching this wonderful large predator hunt is about as exciting as bird watching gets. Young birds of this and other accipiter species have yellow irises that darken with age; the irises of older birds are an intense amber.

RED-SHOULDERED HAWK

Buteo lineatus

The red-shoulder is an uncommon permanent resident and a rare nester. Its habitat is heavily wooded riparian areas, largely along the Mississippi River in eastern Iowa. It suffered a sharp decline as a nester in the 1950s and 1960s but seems to have a stable or even increasing nesting status currently. It often shares its habitat with the barred owl—the owl active by night, the hawk by day. The call of this midsize buteo is one of the few remaining Iowa sounds that drip with wildness.

BROAD-WINGED HAWK

Buteo platypterus

This midsize buteo is a common migrant but a rare nester in Iowa. During migration, it can move in large flocks of two to three thousand birds or more. It nests sparsely across the state, usually in deep woodlands. Iowa birds are gone by mid to late October and are virtually unknown in the state after that.

SWAINSON'S HAWK

Buteo swainsoni

This large buteo is a rare migrant and a very rare nester in Iowa. During migration, it is detected by mid April and is mostly gone after October. It is basically a Great Plains species, and its uncommon nest records occur in the northern and western parts of the state. It sometimes migrates in large flocks, although not as extensive as flocks of the broad-wing. Young Swainson's hawks can be notoriously hard to identify. A field aid is the slight dihedral attitude of the wings when soaring.

J.F.LANDENBERGER

RED-TAILED HAWK

Buteo jamaicensis

Common to abundant throughout the year, this is the bread-and-butter raptor of the bird watcher, yet the four subspecies that occur in Iowa make it a challenge to identify: the western red-tail, the eastern red-tail, Harlan's red-tailed hawk, and Krider's red-tail. With its whitish head and nearly white tail feathers, the Krider's (see page x) is the most spectacular. It apparently formerly nested in Iowa; now it is infrequently seen primarily during migration. Some authors consider it a form, not a full subspecies. The red-tail almost certainly nests in every Iowa county, with the fewest nests in the nearly treeless counties in the northwest. It nests in isolated groves or at the edge of woodlands or even in solitary trees. It nearly always situates its nest so one or more open vistas allow it to hunt or to observe approaching danger.

FERRUGINOUS HAWK

Buteo regalis

One of our rarest raptors, the ferruginous hawk has a nesting range in western Nebraska as its closest approach to Iowa. It is very difficult to positively identify, and many records are not accepted as valid. This is our largest North American buteo.

ROUGH-LEGGED HAWK

Buteo lagopus

This uncommon although regular winter resident arrives in Iowa in late October and leaves by late March. Its nesting range is the Arctic tundra, and its periodic incursions into northern states depend upon the availability of food. A large raptor hovering over an open field in winter is nearly always a rough-leg. Two color phases—dark and light—occur in Iowa; light-phase birds seem to be more common.

GOLDEN EAGLE

Aquila chrysaetos

Here is royalty in the minds of many birders. This western species is a rare migrant and a rare winter resident. Increased observations in recent years are probably due to an increased interest in ornithology but may also reflect increased human activity in its western range. Apparently a few pockets in Iowa, notably along the Upper Iowa and Mississippi rivers in Allamakee County, have been traditional wintering areas for golden eagles since at least the mid 1800s.

AMERICAN KESTREL

Falco sparverius

This small falcon, often called a sparrow hawk, is common as a summer resident, less so as a winter resident, and often abundant during migration. The Iowa Department of Natural Resources, in conjunction with the Iowa Department of Transportation, initiated a nest box program along interstate highways in the early 1980s, and it is now common to see this species hovering over grassy ditches in pursuit of prey or perched on highway signs.

MERLIN

Falco columbarius

The midsize merlin is a rare migrant and a rare winter resident, first occurring during migration in late March and again in late August. A few very old nesting records exist. Two subspecies of this falcon occur in Iowa: the taiga merlin and the Richardson's or prairie merlin, a pale form.

GYRFALCON

Falco rusticolus

The largest of the North American falcons lives mainly in the Arctic; it is of accidental occurrence in Iowa, with fewer than ten documented reports. The first acceptable records, from 1992 and 1993, were of gray-phase immature birds.

PEREGRINE FALCON

Falco peregrinus

The crow-size peregrine falcon is uncommon during migration but is becoming more common due to a reintroduction program started by the Iowa Department of Natural Resources. Falconers, who were at the heart of the reintroduction efforts, led the way toward unlocking the secrets of captive propagation of this and other raptor species. After an absence of some thirty years, natural nesting in historic sites is now occurring.

PRAIRIE FALCON

Falco mexicanus

Records of this rare winter resident come mostly from the western half of Iowa. Observations span from very late August through very late April. This is another Great Plains species that wanders into Iowa after the nesting season. It rarely engages in the spectacular stoops of the peregrine falcon but operates much closer to the ground, often tail-chasing its prey.

BARN OWL

Tyto alba

The barn owl has tough sledding in Iowa because we are at the very northern edge of its range. Too bad, because it is one of our most interesting owls. Nearly worldwide in distribution, it is very beneficial to farmers, to orchardists, and to humans in general since its large broods require a constant supply of food. The state's release program met with limited success because of less-than-ideal habitat conditions probably related to climate change; however, a nest box program for this owl is working.

EASTERN SCREECH-OWL

Megascops asio

The eastern screech-owl has been a fairly common permanent resident. However, records from the current Breeding Bird Atlas Project suggest that its numbers are declining. Whoever named this owl apparently did not hear its tremulous, descending, haunting warble or whinny, which is certainly not a screech; its lonely call also smacks of mystery and Halloween spookiness. The two main color phases—rufous and gray—seem to be nearly equally distributed in Iowa. One of our most beneficial birds, the screech-owl responds well to placement of nest boxes, and recorded calls played during surveys evoke good responses, implying that there may be many more owls than casual observations reveal.

J.F. LANDENBERGER

GREAT HORNED OWL

Bubo virginianus

This common permanent resident and common nester is one of our most efficient predators. It likely nests in every Iowa county because it utilizes a variety of nest structures, preys on a wide variety of birds and mammals, and is not bothered by the presence of humans and human habitation. Its low, melodious call—common in Iowa—is often heard in movies when a spooky night scene is required. Occasionally individuals of the very pale northern subspecies are found as far south as central Iowa.

SNOWY OWL

Bubo scandiacus

The snowy is a rare winter visitor but is present in our state every year. It arrives as early as October and is normally gone by late March. Periodically, large invasions occur when lemmings, its principal food base, are in short supply in the Arctic. This is one of the few owls active during daylight.

NORTHERN HAWK OWL
Surnia ulula

This is an accidental visitor to Iowa, with only two accepted records, one from Black Hawk County in 1981 and 1982 and one from Worth County in 2004 and 2005. As its name implies, its general shape and perching attitude are somewhat hawklike.

J.T.LANDENBERGER

BURROWING OWL

Athene cunicularia

The burrowing owl is a Great Plains species that rarely nests in Iowa, and these nests, as expected, are mostly in the western half of the state. It is our only owl that nests underground. In its principal range, it uses prairie dog burrows for its nest; in Iowa, it probably uses badger dens.

BARRED OWL

Strix varia

The booming call of the barred owl is familiar to anyone even slightly interested in birds. Perhaps our least-studied Iowa raptor, it is a fairly common
nester in deep woods, generally in river bottoms, often sharing its habitat
with red-shouldered hawks at different times of the day and night. It occurs
commonly in the east and southeast parts of the state but becomes less often
seen or heard as one travels to the northwest counties.

GREAT GRAY OWL

Strix nebulosa

This very large owl is of accidental occurrence in Iowa. The fact that it is a bird of coniferous old-growth forests puts it in conflict with logging interests. Its conformation is similar to, though larger than, that of the barred owl, but it has yellow instead of brown eyes. Young nonnesting birds can be heard calling from the marginal habitat where they grow up; they compete for prime habitat when they become nesters.

LONG-EARED OWL

Asio otus

The crow-size long-eared owl occurs regularly but nests rarely in Iowa. Since it feeds on mice and uses old crow nests, it is difficult to understand why this owl is so rare here. In winter, conifer stands are good places to find it.

SHORT-EARED OWL

Asio flammeus

This owl is found in Iowa every year, but only a handful of nesting records exist. In Iowa, as with the northern harrier, the short-ear prefers native prairie for nesting; it seems less likely to use restored prairies or Conservation Reserve Program lands for nesting. This implies that it will be a rare summer resident here for the foreseeable future. This species is often active just at dusk.

J.F.LANDENBERGER

NORTHERN SAW-WHET OWL

Aegolius acadicus

This, the smallest owl found in Iowa, is a visitor from farther north; it is reported every year starting in early October. It is not known to nest here. However, it nests close to the northeast corner of Iowa, where there is plenty of favorable habitat. The boreal owl, *Aegolius funereus*, a resident of boreal forests, is a bit bigger than the saw-whet owl, just as tame, and much rarer, with only one record from Iowa: Black Hawk County in November 2004. This bird was swept in with the dramatic owl invasion that occurred in northern states in the winter of 2004–05.

THE SPIRAL OF PERFECTION

Jon W. Stravers

THERE ARE THOSE OF US who find a wonderful inspiration in the elegance and beauty of birds, especially in the birds of prey. As Edward O. Wilson has suggested, there is a certain biophilia associated with loving the earth and its environs, and raptors have the ability to capture and reflect that sense of wonder, inspiration, and fondness. As part of the community of raptor enthusiasts and protectors, I have been fortunate to spend my career studying red-shouldered hawk nesting and raptor migration along the Mississippi River in the Driftless region of northeast Iowa, whose rugged landscape missed the influence of the last glacial activity.

Dean Roosa and Jim Bednarz first introduced me to the idea of doing fieldwork on red-shouldered hawks in the floodplain forests along the lower parts of the Yellow River and Sny Magill Creek in northeast Iowa in the spring of 1977. Ever since that first encounter (now thirty-five years later as I write this), I have been chasing these birds, slogging through swampy cathedral forests every spring, searching for clues to their secretive life in an effort to develop a better understanding of how these birds make their way in the world.

When I started studying raptors, I spent a lot of time reading about the significant changes that had taken place in raptor populations in Iowa and throughout the United States. First, the European settlement of the continent brought about the loss of prairie grasslands and other abrupt physical changes to the landscape. Previous to the laws that now protect raptors, many birds of prey were often shot or trapped. Then the use of DDT and other persistent pesticides had a significantly negative impact on raptor populations throughout much of the United States.

Now as I am closing in on my retirement years, I look back on equally dynamic changes that have taken place in raptor populations in the last thirty-five years. After decades of general disdain, there is now a new awareness of the importance of the role of raptors in maintaining a balance in prey populations and also as important environmental indicators.

In the early 1970s, three pieces of legislation produced dramatic changes. The Clean Water Act and the Endangered Species Act were enacted, and the use of DDT was banned in the United States (although it is still manufactured and sold to some developing countries). As a result, water quality improved, and bald eagles, who were mostly absent from Iowa and the United States, displayed a remarkable comeback power: they now nest throughout Iowa. Peregrine falcons have been reintroduced and now successfully claim territories all over the United States, in several cities in Iowa, and along the bluffs of the Upper Mississippi River. Ospreys have also been reintroduced and have become part of the fauna at some of Iowa's natural lakes and artificial reservoirs. Red-shouldered hawk populations, once thought to be on the brink of a population crash in Iowa, now seem to be holding their own and expanding into new breeding territories. Red-tailed hawks, the most versatile and adaptable of the raptors, continue to adapt and be successful.

The raptor world in Iowa still holds some mysteries. For instance, we know there is a history of golden eagles wintering in Iowa, especially in the northeast corner, but we don't know a great deal about this, and their current status is still uncertain. Rough-legged hawks can still be seen wintering in Iowa, but I suspect the number of wintering rough-legs has declined significantly in the last fifty years, and their numbers may still be declining. Likewise, species such as the burrowing owl and the barn owl are still struggling to be a consistent part of the bird life in our state.

After these periods that involved some rather radical changes, both good and bad, it will be interesting to see which of these trends in raptor populations continue in the coming years.

ঙ১৫ঞ

LISTENING TO THE LANGUAGE OF RED-SHOULDERED HAWKS

It was the courtship flight of a pair of red-shouldered hawks on a crisp and chilly day in March that first solidified my interest in raptors and sealed my fate. Floating in the updrafts in an undulating pulse of soaring flight and descending dives, a pair of red-shoulders put on an incredible sky dance along a ridge above the Sny Magill complex just south of the town of McGregor along the Mississippi River. The atmospheric conditions on that day were ideal for flying: High pressure and strong winds allowed the birds to put on an incredible aerodynamic display of speed and grace.

At the time, I did not know exactly what I was watching, but I felt a strong pull to investigate the meaning and purpose of such a display. As I would come to understand, these elaborate courtship rituals are an important part of the raptor life cycle. This behavior occurs only during a brief period in March of each year, and it is an intricate part of the pair-bonding process as the birds approach the nesting period.

The normally secretive red-shouldered hawk inhabits the swampy old growth forest cathedrals along the rivers of Iowa. They are more often heard than seen, even in places where they are common along the Mississippi. Their distinctive two-syllable descending call, a sort of "kee-yaw," echoes through some of Iowa's last wild places.

When seen in the misty sunshine or reflected off the water or in light filtered through the forest canopy, the cinnamon orange breast of the adult red-shoulders is striking. Their contoured wing linings are also distinctive, as are the black and white bands on their tails. These birds often spend much of their time inside the canopied forest, making a habit of not providing a strong visual presence. However, when conditions are perfect, with sunny skies and high pressure, I have seen red-shoulders drift overhead and briefly show their translucent half-moon-shaped wing windows.

Red-shoulders are slightly smaller but more agile than their more common cousin, the red-tailed hawk. This agility in flight allows them to reside in forests where red-tails would be unable to maneuver. I find great satisfaction in the fact that they keep coming back to these very same habitats each spring. In some cases, they return to the very same nest tree. I had one nest site just below the Turkey River confluence and just above the town of North Buena Vista where red-shoulders used the same nest tree for thirteen consecutive years. In the Sny Magill complex along the Mississippi River, I have found red-shoulders nesting each and every year since 1977. The nest location may switch around a bit from year to year, but there is always an active red-shoulder nest down at Sny Magill.

Red-shouldered hawks are also a wonderful indicator species, since they normally nest only in large tracts of mature floodplain forests, where there is often a significant collection of other birds using these same habitats. They are connected to places where we have made good land use decisions—where we have preserved the wildness. Consequently, much of my work takes me into a great national treasure, the Upper Mississippi River National Wildlife and Fish Refuge, which covers a 261-mile stretch of the Mississippi River. I often tell people that if you find the wildest and most difficult section of the refuge to get to, you will probably find a red-shoulder nesting there. On the other hand, in places where floodplain forests have been fragmented or where streams have been channelized, red-shoulders are not to be found. Indeed, they are absent from many parts of Iowa.

Over the years, the way I do the work of finding red-shoulder nests has changed. I spend much more time listening *before* I begin searching. As I work, I listen for the male to announce his displeasure at my presence. He spends a great deal of time patrolling the nesting territory boundaries, and he is likely to be anywhere within the roughly one square kilometer that might be considered his. In general, he is the more vocal of the pair.

More importantly, I listen for the female to call back. It is her call that is usually closer to the nest site—and her call that gives me a better clue where to search. In fact, once you learn how to listen to the red-shoulder language, you can hear the story that she tells throughout the nesting period all the way from courtship, through incubation, and then hatching, and subsequently the fledging of the young. Minute innuendoes within her language hint at each different stage in the nesting cycle.

I have learned other methods of deciphering red-shoulder secrets. In March of 2001, when there was still a layer of crusty snow in the Sny Magill bottoms, after an extended search without hearing or seeing any red-shoulders, I worked my way over to the nest tree the birds had used the previous year. And there, directly below last year's nest, I found a fresh breast feather from an adult red-shoulder curled up on top of the crusty snow. Even though I had not heard or seen a red-shoulder, I knew they were back on territory. Perhaps this feather had been left in the nest, which might be like leaving a note on the kitchen table. "Honey, I am back from winter migration. Right now I am out in the uplands hunting, but I'll be back here later."

On several occasions I have found a gathering of multiple red-shoulders— adults and juveniles all noisy and calling—in various types of flights and obviously participating in some kind of group-oriented behavior. With all of the calling and commotion, I figured that this display had to result in an active nest in the immediate area. In each case I did eventually find active nests in the general vicinity (1 mile north and another 1.5 miles east), but I was unable to subsequently find an active nest centered in the specific area where the gathering had occurred. This puzzled me since my previous experience always led me to believe that if red-shoulders where present and calling in March, there should be an active nest nearby.

It took me several years and three more communal activity events before I began to get a sense of what was actually happening in these gatherings.

Since I have been unable to find anyone who could describe or name this particular activity, I have labeled these events as precourtship communal gatherings, as a "rhouse" of red-shoulders (pronounced like "whose"). I have found these gatherings of multiple birds only during the earliest parts of the nesting season, and I have found them only on the cusp of several active territories. I believe these gatherings are a result both of clumping of active territories and of having enough suitable habitat in the area to maintain several active territories within a given region. Once the nesting season commences, I don't think these gatherings occur; some areas are neutral ground, but when the birds go into nesting and territorial mode, they generally don't invade each other's nesting territories.

These events are most likely an important community function in the local red-shouldered hawk population—like getting together with the neighbors at a certain time of the year. I believe these gatherings function in a social sense to help keep specific territories active. For example, if a particular mate did not survive the winter, the surviving adult might use these gatherings to locate and recruit a new partner (perhaps a bird's idea of a dating service). In addition, during these events the youngster red-shoulders are most likely learning the routines of what it means to be an adult red-shoulder.

Red-shoulders are masters of flying underneath the canopy and through the open subcanopy created by the structure of these older forests. On one occasion, while floating in my flatboat into the confluence of Sny Magill Creek and working my way up the creek, I was startled by a red-shoulder that suddenly bolted from the forest at full speed only inches above the tops of the nettle vegetation and only about two feet off the water. A small flock of common grackles were working the opposite shore. When the red-shoulder burst into the clearing, the grackles squawked loudly as they scattered in all directions, but the hawk targeted one of the grackles and immediately snagged it midair and carried it to a nearby clearing a few yards away. I could hear the grackle protesting desperately, but to no avail, and it was soon quiet. It all happened in just an instant, a few heartbeats.

I think many of us often take the migration of birds each spring and fall for granted, or perhaps we just plain ignore it. On the other hand, human beings have most likely been wondering about bird migration for as long as humans have been humans—or even longer. It can be a mystical experience to watch a golden eagle or a merlin or a broad-winged hawk appear in the northern sky, then drift steadily and magically overhead and off to the south in a matter of a few minutes. In a brief moment the bird has covered the entire distance one can see. This type of scene always captures my heart and soul; I have been making a ritual of autumn migration season for half of my life.

In 1976, I began working on raptor migration studies with Dean Roosa. We ran a modest banding station in a hayfield on the hills in Allamakee County, just north of Wexford Creek in northeast Iowa. We continued our efforts to understand and define raptor migration through this region in the following years. Then, in the autumn of 1982, with support from the Iowa Conservation Commission, we established a day-to-day monitoring of autumn raptor migration through this region. With some help from the staff at Effigy Mounds National Monument, we established a raptor banding station in the south unit of Effigy. We found that some days had significant numbers of migrating raptors and other days hardly any or even no migration at all. And each day there were periods of moderate movement and periods when we found hardly any movement whatsoever. Raptor migration is greatly influenced by the overall regional weather pattern, and their movements also resemble the weather—constantly changing, with no idea what to expect.

A couple of years later, in 1984, the Wildlife Diversity Program of the Iowa Department of Natural Resources helped initiate HawkWatch Weekend at Effigy Mounds National Monument. This event celebrates the migration of birds and our connection to the planet through birds and their marvelous flights. And now, many years later with the help of a variety of people and organizations, we are still celebrating the migration of raptors through our region on the first weekend in October at Effigy Mounds.

We Iowans do not get to witness some of the biggest concentrations of raptor migration that can occur in some regions of the planet. In Veracruz, Mexico, and in Costa Rica and Panama, for example, a person can see thousands of raptors in the sky at once—as many as 10,000 in an hour or 80,000 in a day. It is a spectacle that has to be experienced in order to be fully believed.

Even though we may not get to witness those incredible concentrations of raptors in Iowa, we do have areas where raptors often follow certain landforms, like the Loess Hills in western Iowa or the Mississippi River through the Driftless region in northeast Iowa. Here, raptors often use these topographic features as a sort of leading line.

In northeast Iowa, the rock bluffs deflect the winds and create favorable updrafts while the pockets of thermally heated air rise out of the valleys during midday. These favorable wind conditions actually help raptors do the work of migration. At the same time, the north-south linear nature of the Mississippi River Valley creates a favorable leading line that the birds follow in various manners. In addition, the forested slopes provide favorable resting and night-roosting habitat for many migrating birds.

All of these conditions together result in the Driftless area being prominent in raptor migration, as it has probably been for eons. These migrating raptors are in fact a visual link to ancestral populations. It is quite possible that when we watch an Arctic peregrine falcon or a Cooper's hawk migrating along the Mississippi River Valley, we are watching the descendants of a population that has been doing this same migration year after year, decade after decade, century after century.

Raptor migration projects have grown in many regions of North America. Results from these studies have helped to monitor changes in raptor populations and also build a more complete picture of the timing of raptor movements and how those movements are tied to regional and continental weather patterns. The red-tailed hawk you see floating overhead during the noon hour on a crisp October day has been influenced by the previous day's weather north of us, and this bird most likely already has some kind of sense of the type of weather it will face tomorrow when it is 60 or 150 miles further south.

Through these migration monitoring projects, we may be learning some of the details of where certain raptor species are going, or where they are leaving from, but there are still a great many unanswered questions about how they are able to make their way back to specific locations after making an incredibly long journey each autumn and then again in the following spring. We have learned that migration and winter often take a regular toll on the raptor populations, since a significant portion of any population fails to survive their first winter.

ᴔᴄᴛᴇ

TALES FROM THE BANDING STATION

In my thirty-plus years of banding raptors, I have had a variety of unforgettable experiences. Banding often involves long periods of sitting and waiting quietly in the hawk blind. The boredom of this waiting is inevitably interspersed with brief periods of intense activity as birds appear high in the sky and then sometimes fly full speed with reckless abandon into the banding station, making those periods of boredom worth the wait.

Four famous birds from our banding station in northeast Iowa have yielded some interesting information. One of these was a young sharp-shinned hawk that we banded along the Mississippi River during her autumn migration in 1992. Later that winter, the bird was accidentally electrocuted in the northern portion of Costa Rica (not far from where my daughter Lisa would eventually serve in the Peace Corps).

One of the most startling experiences occurred in 1983, when Dave McIlrath captured a young peregrine falcon that had been banded as a nestling that previous summer in the Sondre Stromfjord region of Greenland. Some of the peregrine experts said that all the peregrines from Greenland were migrating along the eastern coast of the United States, but they apparently did not give this particular piece of information to this specific bird.

A second exciting falcon showed up in 1999 during HawkWatch Weekend at Effigy Mounds, when I captured an adult female peregrine falcon that had been banded four years earlier as a nestling along the Tanana River in central Alaska.

The last famous bird was a Cooper's hawk that we captured in October of 2004. This bird had originally been banded by Ernesto Ruelas (a friend of mine) at his banding station in the state of Veracruz in Mexico four years earlier, in October of 2000. What makes this such a wonderful experience is that I had worked with Ernesto in the autumn of 1989 at a HawkWatch International banding station in the Goshute Mountains of Nevada. Along with other raptor biologists, we had given Ernesto some initial ideas about creating a raptor migration monitoring program near his home in Veracruz. When Ernesto returned to Veracruz he helped to set up what eventually became a world-famous raptor migration spectacle—one of those places where you can see 10,000 raptors an hour.

๛

A LIFE BUILT AROUND RAPTORS

As my son Jon Jr. grew up, he thought studying raptor nesting and capturing raptors during the autumn migration were normal things to do. By the time he was eleven, he had learned how to record data at hawk nests we were studying and how to safely handle raptors at our autumn migration banding station. As a nineteen-year-old, Jon-Jon started working for HawkWatch International at migration projects in the western United States. His focus and resolve inside the trapping blind were always more intense than my own. Adapting Ralph Waldo Emerson's guideline that "the measure of mental health is the disposition to find good everywhere" to his own world, he lived with the belief that "the measure of spiritual health is the disposition to find a raptor anywhere."

As he found his way to build a life around raptor studies, Jon-Jon worked on a variety of field research projects: on golden eagles nesting in the Snake River Birds of Prey Natural Area in Idaho for the Bureau of Land Management, on northern goshawk nesting in Oregon for the U.S. Forest Service, on peregrine falcon nesting in the Grand Canyon for the National Park Service, on ferruginous hawk and golden eagle nesting in the intermountain plains of New Mexico for Hawks Aloft. And, while working on a willow flycatcher nesting study along streams in southern Arizona, he took the time to document and study gray hawk and zone-tailed hawk nesting, two of the rarest nesting hawks in the United States.

Jon-Jon had a marvelous ability to appreciate the beauty of raptors and the adaptive behavior that allowed each species to be successful. He became astute at understanding the subtle differences between accipiter populations from southern deserts and those from northern mountain forests. As his understanding of raptor populations in the natural world expanded, he became the teacher and I became the student.

ॐ

A MATTER OF ETERNAL VIGILANCE

As these years in the field have gone by, I have counted myself as one of the most fortunate to have been able to work with raptors. To watch a peregrine falcon swoop across the face of a rock bluff along the Mississippi River is to witness true grace and speed connected to the sacred beauty of a rock escarpment that has occupied this space for millions of years.

Listening to a pair of red-shouldered hawks call to each other from deep inside a forest along the Upper Mississippi River is listening to the sacred language of wildness. And to witness the reckless abandon of a goshawk darting full speed toward a pigeon in our autumn banding station is a new take on the word "sudden." Watching a pair of bald eagles building their nest and then watching as these birds add to and use this same nest and raise young eagles every year for the next twelve years makes me feel part of their story.

All these and a thousand other episodes are treasured gifts that I received for choosing to study and live with raptors.

Raptors have shown a great strength and a marvelous ability to adapt and survive. At the same time the lessons in the use of DDT and the loss of habitat have shown that raptors can be totally vulnerable and acutely sensitive to negative influences in the environment. I hope future Iowans will always find the time in their busy lives to stop and watch and enjoy the beauty and grace of the spiral of perfection in a hawk when it soars. I also hope future Iowans will have the resolve, the ingenuity, and the consciousness to be totally aware of what is happening to raptor populations in their state. As Gladys Black used to say, "It is a matter of eternal vigilance."

ACKNOWLEDGMENTS

For the last three decades I have been fortunate to be able to work on a variety of bird-monitoring projects supported by various agencies including the U.S. Fish and Wildlife Service (several districts of the Upper Mississippi Refuge), the U.S. Army Corps of Engineers Mississippi River Natural Resources Section, the Iowa Department of Natural Resources Wildlife Diversity Program, and Effigy Mounds National Monument. I am also grateful to the National Audubon Society's chapters throughout Iowa. They were the first to support my work, and their collective and continued support provided some of the matching funds that have made a significant difference in keeping some of these raptor monitoring projects alive over time. The National Audubon Society's Mississippi River Initiative has also been instrumental in keeping me on the river and working with the birds.

I am also grateful to have known James Landenberger. I was always in awe of the detail he incorporated into his paintings. I am sorry that he is not with us to celebrate this publication of his memorable paintings.

Perhaps most importantly for the future health of our raptors are the people who have gotten involved in these hawk-migration and hawk-nesting projects. Some of them came for a short time and enjoyed their experience. Some contributed in unique ways in order to keep these projects going. And some, like Dave Kester, made significant changes in their lives in order to keep coming back to work on these and other projects year after year.

These folks are in fact part of what I call the Gladys Tree in reference to Gladys Black, the Bird Lady of Iowa. Without the initial encouragement and training that Gladys gave me in the mid 1970s, none of this would have happened, and I will be forever grateful to her. And now, in a certain sense I get to be Gladys in the lives of other young birders. Her influence lives on.

A GROWING APPRECIATION FOR RAPTORS

Bruce Ehresman

THE SLOW METAMORPHOSIS in the attitude of Iowans—and the larger society—toward raptors appears to be one of the greatest factors facilitating the restoration of populations of a growing number of these predatory bird species. Undoubtedly, some of the credit for this transformation is due to those who have been involved with environmental education by promoting the virtues of raptors. Events begun decades ago, like HawkWatch Weekends, Bald Eagle Appreciation Days, and Owl Prowls, allow tens of thousands of citizens each year to more personally experience these magnificent birds. Perhaps this change of attitude is also due to the fact that most people now grow up in towns and cities: They have not grown up believing that predator birds threaten the existence of the many types of domestic livestock that once were prevalent outdoors throughout Iowa. Regardless of the cause of the improved public attitude toward raptors, those of us who find our days and nights brightened by the presence of these birds are most grateful for this shift in consciousness.

While it is important to credit environmental educators for their role in aiding raptor populations' recovery, credit is also due to the wildlife biologists and a cadre of raptor enthusiasts who made it a high priority to return several raptor species that had been eliminated, or nearly so, from nesting in the Iowa landscape. In the 1970s, Iowa's state ecologist, Dean Roosa, played a major role in collecting scientific data about Iowa's endangered, threatened, and extirpated—eliminated as breeders—species. He then suggested that restoration programs be created to bring some of these species back. Dave Newhouse, Iowa's first Department of Natural Resources nongame biologist, wrote a Barn Owl Restoration Plan, and the first of several Iowa raptor restoration and reintroduction efforts was underway.

From 1983 to 1987, nearly five hundred barn owls were reared in captivity and released at forty-four sites in twenty-eight counties, mostly in concerned citizens' barns and other outbuildings where barn owls had been prevalent several decades earlier. Radio transmitters placed on thirty-six of the released barn owls allowed researchers to learn that great horned owls were the main predator of this smaller species and that very few released barn owls survived. Still, twenty-five years later, efforts to maintain an Iowa barn owl population are paying off, and a nest box program for this species is working. Most years, about five barn owl nests are reported in the state, especially in southern counties where some grassland remains.

Even though the barn owl restoration effort has not been as successful as hoped, Iowa's next restoration effort has been. The widespread use of organochlorine pesticides led to the elimination of peregrine falcon nesting on the Mississippi River bluffs in the early to mid 1960s; by that time no more peregrines nested from Iowa to the east coast. Iowa joined a larger effort, the Midwest Peregrine Falcon Restoration Project, and in 1989 began hacking (a soft-release technique that includes providing the birds with food) peregrines from sites on tall buildings in large urban areas. From 1989 to 1992, fifty young peregrines were released from four different sites. This effort resulted in the first successful peregrine nests in three decades in 1993 and the establishment of three different nest sites, one each in Cedar Rapids, Des Moines, and Davenport. Each of these three peregrine territories is still active today.

By the mid 1990s, it was apparent to those of us involved with this reintroduction project that more peregrines should be released on or near the Mississippi River to encourage nesting in the historic eyries—the nesting sites—on the cliff faces lining the river. Fortunately for Iowa, Bob Anderson, who was breeding peregrines for the Midwest Peregrine Falcon Restoration Project at that time, moved to Iowa to help lead this Mississippi River bluffs restoration effort. An Iowa Peregrine Falcon Recovery Team was formed, and Iowa's Peregrine Falcon Recovery Plan was revised by Iowa DNR Wildlife Technician Pat Schlarbaum. Former Iowa DNR employee and master falconer Lowell Washburn, as well as the Iowa Falconer's Association, also played a key role in this restoration effort. Approximately 110 more peregrines were raised and released into the wild, and as a result of this effort, peregrine falcons are now nesting in historic eyries on Mississippi River bluffs in Iowa, Minnesota, and Wisconsin. Bob Anderson and his associate, Dave Kester, continue to monitor, band, and create potential nest sites for peregrines on the big river. Statewide, in 2012, there are sixteen peregrine nest sites (there were perhaps ten nest sites historically), and this species is no longer listed as either state or federally endangered or threatened.

Another species associated with the Mississippi River (and other rivers) bears mentioning. The red-shouldered hawk was another casualty of the DDT era, but it seems to be staging a recovery of its own. While other researchers brought attention to the poor status of this species in Iowa several decades ago, it has been the longstanding effort of Jon Stravers to study this species and inform the public of the importance of protecting and maintaining the wild places that this charismatic and handsome hawk calls home. During Iowa's first Breeding Bird Atlas Project in the late 1980s, most nesting pairs of red-shouldered hawks were found in Allamakee and Clayton counties in floodplain forests along the Mississippi River. During Iowa's current Breeding Bird Atlas Project, this species has been found in forty-three counties, with nesting confirmed in sixteen counties. Growing populations are being documented in most major watersheds in the eastern two-thirds of Iowa. While still listed as endangered in Iowa, if the red-shoulder's growing population trend continues, it should be removed from Iowa's Endangered/Threatened Species List in the near future. Jon's effort to teach wildlife managers and fellow conservationists about the type of habitat that this species requires has reaped dividends. Today's wildlife managers are doing a much better job of considering the habitat needs of red-shouldered hawks, as well as many other nongame (that is, nonhunted) wildlife that likely were given little if any consideration a few decades ago.

The species' recovery that blows the doors off all other raptor recoveries is the bald eagle. No bald eagle nests were known in this state from 1906 through 1976. In 2012 there appear to be more than three hundred active nesting territories within, at least, ninety-three of Iowa's ninety-nine counties. To put this species' recovery in perspective, Iowa now holds two-thirds as many eagle nests as existed in the entire lower forty-eight states in 1963. While outlawing use of DDT in this country in 1973 was a major coup for this species, so were other federal laws, like the Bald and Golden Eagle Protection Act and the Endangered Species Act. But even with these protective laws, I suspect no one could have predicted the huge population recovery that this species has shown. Iowa's recovery goal was to have ten active nests by the year 2000; there were at least one hundred nests that year!

Certainly there were widespread efforts in the 1980s and 1990s to assure that every active Iowa eagle nest was protected and watched over, but it was particularly encouraging to discover that this species was apparently adapting to living in close proximity to humans. Numerous eagle nest trees in Iowa are located within fifty yards of people's homes or outbuildings. At least two are located above parking areas at boat ramps. It appears that eagles are adapting to human activity. Perhaps a mutual benefit has grown out of this relationship, since most people who have eagle nests on their property are absolutely delighted. The world-famous Decorah nesting eagles that are featured on Bob

Anderson's webcam certainly seem to have improved the status of the bald eagle as well.

The most recent bird of prey to become targeted for reintroduction to Iowa is the osprey. While no confirmed nest records exist in Euro-American documents, Native Americans' oral traditions express knowledge of this bird's existence in northwest Iowa, especially in the larger lakes in Dickinson County. The Macbride Raptor Project, under the leadership of Jodeane Cancilla, first released juvenile ospreys in Johnson County in 1997. The osprey release effort resulted in Iowa's first documented nesting attempt in 2000; the first successful nest was in 2003. Pat Schlarbaum oversees Iowa's Osprey Restoration Program, but a great deal of the credit for this program's success rests with its myriad of volunteers and local osprey release site coordinators. Through 2011, 266 ospreys, relocated from wild nests in both Wisconsin and Minnesota, have been released at eleven hack sites in eleven Iowa counties. In 2011, there were sixteen active Iowa nest sites. In a few more years, Iowa should have a large enough reproducing population to sustain itself, and no more releases of ospreys will be necessary. At one time, fully two-thirds of Wisconsin's osprey population nested on artificial platforms, evidence of this species' proclivity for nesting on human-made structures.

One feisty little raptor who is easily enticed to nest in artificial structures is the American kestrel. Like many other raptor species at that time, this small falcon's population numbers were very low in the early 1980s. To address that apparent population decline, now-retired Iowa DNR Wildlife Biologist Ron Andrews, with the blessing of the Iowa Department of Transportation, began placing kestrel nest boxes on the back of signs along Interstate 35 in 1983. By the late 1990s, well over a thousand kestrel nest boxes lined Iowa's roadways, and conservationists were banding nearly eight hundred young kestrels each year in those nest boxes. Most years about two-thirds of all nest boxes placed were used by nesting kestrels. Because Iowa's program has been so successful, at least twenty-five other states and several other countries have now adopted Iowa's model and initiated roadside kestrel nest box programs of their own.

While the above species have benefitted from human helping hands, other Iowa birds of prey appear to be suffering from dwindling populations. For instance, for the Swainson's hawk, current records from Iowa's Breeding Bird Atlas Project indicate more than a 50 percent reduction in records from atlas work done in the 1980s. A worse scenario exists for the eastern screech-owl: 69 percent fewer records have been collected during the current atlas survey than during the first one. Obviously, these examples highlight the importance of monitoring bird populations to keep track of their health. The next step will be for someone to research why these raptor species may be declining.

Iowa is blessed to have many different conservation organizations and several conservation agencies. Each of these organizations and agencies has a different purpose or mission, but each plays an important role by concentrating on environmental education and promoting an improved Iowa conservation ethic. (Aldo Leopold referred to this ethic as an environmental conscience.) One group, in particular, that seems to reach people's hearts is wildlife rehabilitators. While conservation agencies, like the Iowa DNR, focus their efforts on sustaining populations of animals, wildlife rehabilitators focus mostly on individuals. Wildlife rehabilitators, in particular, reach people who relate best to individual animals. Since many people find it difficult to relate to wildlife populations, relating to individuals within those populations provides an important conduit to caring about wildlife in general. Once people care about wildlife in general, they are much more likely to be advocates for the well-being of those animals. The fact that Iowa already has lost a higher percentage of wildlife habitat than any other state in the country says much about the importance of caring for the dwindling numbers of remaining wildlife and the habitats that support them.

ACKNOWLEDGMENTS

Without the cadre of dedicated volunteers who provide the backbone for most of the raptor restoration efforts, far fewer of each of Iowa's rarer raptor species would nest here. Many of these same people continue to monitor nest sites and count wintering raptors as well, which allows conservation agencies to track the health of these species' populations. These gracious people deserve the gratitude of all who feel they cannot properly live without the presence of wildness.

I am indebted to numerous mentors, including Fran Hamerstrom and Gladys Black, who both held raptors in very high esteem. But it is people like Dean Roosa and Jon Stravers who most inspired me to become a raptor enthusiast. For many years, my wife, Marlene, and I participated in a Winter Raptor Survey that Dean coordinated for the state. Then I began helping Jon monitor red-shouldered hawk nests in northeast Iowa. I became hooked on raptors, and my involvement with the programs and projects already described strengthened that attachment. I will never tire of seeing cute little white fuzz-ball peregrine falcons in a nest, watching a rehabilitated barred owl fly back to the woods after its broken wing has been repaired, or hearing the raucous cry of a bald eagle warning intruders to stay away from its nest.

Many years ago, while traveling with Dean and Jon to Cedar Rapids to meet with Jim Landenberger to discuss the possibility of writing essays to go with his wonderful raptor paintings, I witnessed firsthand how much respect Dean and Jon have for birds of prey. Spotting a red-tailed hawk perched in a tree on the roadside, Dean stopped the car so that we could admire the bird. Dean smiled up at the red-tail and said, "Isn't it magnificent?" We all agreed that it was indeed magnificent. To this day, as a result of that encounter, I often find myself saluting or nodding to raptors as I pass them by. How fortunate I am to be able to work with raptors and with the people who care so deeply about their future.

The Emerald Horizon: The History of Nature in Iowa
By Cornelia F. Mutel

Enchanted by Prairie
By Bill Witt and Osha Gray Davidson

Fifty Common Birds of the Upper Midwest
Watercolors by Dana Gardner, text by Nancy Overcott

Fifty Uncommon Birds of the Upper Midwest
Watercolors by Dana Gardner, text by Nancy Overcott

Forest and Shade Trees of Iowa: Third Edition
By Peter van der Linden and Donald Farrar

Fragile Giants: A Natural History of the Loess Hills
By Cornelia F. Mutel

An Illustrated Guide to Iowa Prairie Plants
By Paul Christiansen and Mark Müller

The Iowa Breeding Bird Atlas
By Laura Spess Jackson, Carol A. Thompson, and James J. Dinsmore

The Iowa Lakeside Laboratory: A Century of Discovering the Nature of Nature
By Michael J. Lannoo

Landforms of Iowa
By Jean C. Prior

Man Killed by Pheasant and Other Kinships
By John T. Price

Of Men and Marshes
By Paul L. Errington

Out Home
By John Madson

A Practical Guide to Prairie Reconstruction
By Carl Kurtz

Prairie: A North American Guide
By Suzanne Winckler

Stories from under the Sky
By John Madson

A Tallgrass Prairie Alphabet
By Claudia McGehee

Up on the River: People and Wildlife of the Upper Mississippi
By John Madson

The Vascular Plants of Iowa: An Annotated Checklist and Natural History
By Lawrence J. Eilers and Dean M. Roosa

A Watershed Year: Anatomy of the Iowa Floods of 2008
Edited by Cornelia F. Mutel

Where Do Birds Live?
By Claudia McGehee

Where the Sky Began: Land of the Tallgrass Prairie
By John Madson

Wildflowers and Other Plants of Iowa Wetlands
By Sylvan T. Runkel and Dean M. Roosa

Wildflowers of Iowa Woodlands
By Sylvan T. Runkel and Alvin F. Bull

Wildflowers of the Tallgrass Prairie: The Upper Midwest
By Sylvan T. Runkel and Dean M. Roosa

A Woodland Counting Book
By Claudia McGehee

This book was designed and typeset in Chapparal Pro with
Chase display and Rustic Sage Ornaments by Kristina Kachele Design, llc.
It was printed on 70 lb. Gusto Satin paper at Versa Press, Inc., in Peoria, Illinois.